Maybe

MAYBE

Appley UK Publishing
www.appleyuk.com

ISBN: 9781549971341

We have all experienced that feeling,
when the shroud of sadness falls heavily
over us

The desolate and empty feeling that grips
every tragic breath you take.

As spiralling self doubt, why, why,
silently eats your existence and reason
for living away.

From this despair, I will open my
angry fists, that have wiped away
too many tears, to hold a pen that
will write these words, to
renew hope
That I will love again.

Maybe

Maybe
a word full of hope
maybe its all about you
maybe it isn't
maybe you'll read
and understand
maybe one day
you'll be here

just maybe.

Why I write

I write
for my sanity
and for you.

If i get over you

I stared at the text you sent me, again,
asking how I was.

Few months after.

I stared unable to form a sentence or
two.
Thinking what it would feel like to be
over you
I wondered if we had never met,
how it would be like
where would I be?

I wanted to not to reply to you,
but I wasn't over you

I will stop, If i get over you.

Lonely street

There is no beat
in the heart
of lonely street

All over again

I don't want you back
I really don't
but I would love to
go back again
to the night we met
for the feeling
of meeting you all over again

go back to us being strangers

just for meeting you
all over again
well, I'd give the world.

My time

You were always late
so I found something better
to do with my time

Cold

You are cold as the ice
That chills your veins
And slippery in your deceit
With a heart that does not melt
Even on the warmest of occasions

I tried to teach you the ways of love
Only for you to leave me
Forgotten and helpless
On your carpet of frost

It was understandable the icicle
Would be your weapon of choice
To pierce my heart.

Blankets

Cover me with blankets
of stars and moons
so I can sparkle and shine
through the darkness
that was you

Promises

One more try
and
I'll get it right
this time
I promise

"Don't make promises you cant keep" He said

I need an instruction manual

Almost
I loved you
guess I didn't know how to

Memories and silhouettes

Across chilled marble floors
our memories and silhouettes
Still dance under darkened veils
Spectres of the night
Restless like howling winds
Shadows in the moonlight
Reflections of something
That once resembled
Happiness.

Wondering

For forever
I'll wonder why

why we didn't last
why did you leave

Overthoughts

My thoughts were with
all those things
you never said

A puzzle

We were a puzzle
a jigsaw
with a missing
piece

Wind

I asked you
"would you love me as the seasons change?"
you smiled and hugged me

maybe I didn't hear the "no"

as the leaves fell and
disappeared with the wind
you did too.

Since you

How are you?

Three simple words
became the hardest
to answer

since you

About you,
about him

I'll drink wine with my new best friend
while we laugh at our inside jokes

I'll tell her about you, she'll tell
me about him.
we will think of texting, but we won't
Instead
we will drink more wine and flirt with
the guys there

we will remember on our way home;
All about you, all about him
and we will confess things that the
wine makes us confess.
we will sit on a floor at 3am
with a tear in our eyes

and then laugh
our hearts out.

Another shot

I took a shot of vodka
and then three more
while sitting on the wood floors
in my apartment
thinking of texting you
asking how you've been
asking if you would
love me again

Things I'll do when I miss you

I'll eat lots of chocolate and then text my
friend. Telling her that I miss you.
She'll tell me something to get my mind of you.
I'll miss you after 5 minutes, again.
I'll look at your pictures
I'll wonder what you are doing,
where you are and who you are with.
I'll text another,
but he isn't you.
I'll be thinking about texting you.
but I wont.
I'll listen to a song that reminds me
of you, I'll listen more
I'll imagine us
I'll write until my hands hurt
I'll write until I have no words left anymore
I'll write
I'll check my phone to see if you have texted.
You haven't
I'll put my phone back, with the screen down.

and somehow fall asleep
dreaming of you.

Just friends

It all started with a smile
and ended with a kiss

all those conversations from morning till 3am,
we never said bye, we carried on our
meaningless but meaningful talks,
all those long walks that went for miles without
a destination, but a journey for us,
all those laughter and miles for no reason
just because we were around each other,
just hearing your name made me smile
we always found a way just to be the two of us

guess we got confused, guess it was all just
because
we were friends,
just friends

I am just a friend to you and you are just a
friend to me
just friends is all that we would ever be

Thieves in the night

Like thieves in the night
we stole moments from each other
that can never
be returned, repeated or forgotten.

After that night

The moon was out
we had left the bar
where we shared a few glasses of wine
and conversation

we filled the dark, empty streets
with laughter and carelessness.
rose tints painted our cheeks
with a giggle in our eyes
where we looked at each other
and shared a kiss

after that night
we shared many things
somehow we couldn't quite share
our lives.

Scar

I had this scar on my hand
when I met you

you asked about it
and touched it softly.
after it always reminded me of you
and made me smile
I didn't hate it anymore.

but it's gone now
just like you

Separate paths

You changed a lot, you did
you became like a dream
that disappears every morning
only waiting for me at night.

you didn't look at what you
had left behind
you left behind something that
is hard to get rid of.

unanswered questions are what
is left behind from you
one thing was for sure
we always walked separate paths.

All her dreams

The red eyed girl in the bathroom, pops another pill.
another day of boredom, searching for a thrill.
the postman brings more junk mail,
that piles up on the floor
It doesn't really matter, she's not going out the door.

snowstorm on the tv, books are never read
her eyes are glazed and lonely,
as she lays upon her bed
the scars upon her wrists, are stories of regret
of people she once knew, and those she never met.

never going out, never having fun
never knows which way to turn, or how her life will run
she's made so many lists, of what she wanted to do
and one by one, all her dreams fell through.

he left her long ago, left her high and dry
so now she's selling tickets to watch her life go by
he was never interested, he didn't even care
she thought it was love, but to him just a brief affair.

My angry heart

My angry heart
bruised and alone
a beat fast and furious
as the wires of my veins
pull tight in frustration
why
why did you break me

Always another

I thought you were the
guy of my dreams

I woke up now

it was a good dream
at the time

it's morning again

you weren't the one
you were just a
one.

Better than you

I feel an icy chill as you pass me in the street
I feel so uncomfortable every time we meet
I'll tell you now as i've told you before
Your face doesn't fit round here anymore

here's my put down like the words of a song
you hurt me so bad, you did so much wrong
I know it was true, I was better than you
So much better, better than you

Once the perfect boy but left a bitter taste
should have thought things through, not rushed in haste
should have ended before we walked hand in hand
to say last goodbyes with a one last night stand

always so well informed, trying to be smart
I wondered how you'll do now we've grown apart
the hands on the clock says its much too late
we've gone on too long past our sell by date.

Reflection

Every time I look in a mirror
I still see your reflection
reflecting on what you are now missing

Fragments

Those moments we shared
that were so tender
are now just
fragments of time frozen
a bitter chill
that stills my heart

I knew you, briefly

Someone said your name today
I got lost in my thoughts for a minute
then I smiled, remembering and looked
at the person and said
I knew him, briefly
and smiled again, knowing that briefly meant

the way your eyes smiled when you ate your favourite
cake
the way your dimples appeared when I made you laugh
the way you would bite your pinky which annoyed me then
the way you'd sing along to your favourite song on the
radio
the way you'd rest your head on my lap after a long day
the way you'd go on about the sky, the stars and the
universe

the way we were
the way we loved

I knew you, briefly

Your name

Your name appearing on the screen of my
phone
made my heart jump,
you still had that effect on me.

hearing your name from friends, made me listen
to what'll come out after.
without showing that I still care.

but I did, I still do.

and I wonder how you feel when you see
my name on your screen
or
When someone mentions my name

A love now gone

Even though our music
has long since faded
into the dark and restless night
I still dance to the rhythm and beats
of our broken hearts
holding on to the melodies
and memories
of a love now gone

Wounds

Your jaundiced views
are wounds
that will never
heal

Answer of you

I'm still leaving clues
to the answer of you

Spinning top

Feeling out my heartbeat
your laughter sounds so false
smiling at the scent you wear
that tried to drive my pulse
the glass of wine I'm drinking
speaks inside my head
the words that spill out from it
are words better not said

we used to love each other
now there's only pain
shivers running down my spine
have frozen me again
fears turn into tears
that pour into the night
so walk away its over
you know that I am right

like a spinning top
the colours blur
as your words keep ringing
through my mind
it's always the lies
that hurt
always the lies
that hurt you

Lost

I got too lost in you
and now
I can't find my way

The lies she told

She said she was fine
that she can handle it
she said she is over it
that she's getting there

she said she's losing the parts of you
but she had turned
                    into you
                    herself

And her

"So why didn't you ever call him?"
I asked her
She lit a cigarette
inhaled
and let the smoke out

"I couldn't" She finally said

She told me many years had
passed by.
Many seasons

He had changed now
he wasn't into Spring
anymore
he had moved on to
Summer now

And her? She was still in Winter

Stolen

Your lipstick smeared
by razor blades
a crimson tapestry
of your own design
cutting deep
mocking
at what was once
intimate moments
now stolen
dying in your arms
is no longer an option

I left

And I left
I finally decided to leave
I know, I wasn't expecting it either
guess you'll believe my unpredictability after all

I left the past, our memories and you
I couldn't wait for you to decide anymore
I hope you realise, its not my decision
it was yours.

Changes

You only knew me in
one moment in life

a time that came and went
away with the seasons

seasons change

I've changed with them.

Timing

We always blame the timing
when things don't work out

no such thing as
wrong time

it just wasn't meant
to last

But we cant live with an if

I loved you two seasons
ago
but I am changing with
the seasons
I still miss you sometimes
like rain, that appears
every season

but seasons change
and I will too

last spring I was different
and next spring
I'll be different
but what if i never get over you

Its not me

I promise
I do
that someone will
love you
a lot
but that someone
is not me

I can't stay

Too short

Is there a plan made for us
by the universe
I don't know
maybe I could figure it out
but the thing is
life is too short
and we only have now
there might be no time
to live with a maybe

I was actually sure
still am
that we would meet again
maybe we will soon
but now i'm leaving
a parallel road
maybe our paths will cross again
but life is too short
to live with a maybe

Forever falling

Forever falling
through the ice on my
lake of frozen teardrops

Moved on

And in a heartbeat
I have already
moved on

There always is

It's 2pm when I'll remember
you.
I might still be waiting for a text
or a call
or any sign
maybe that wont happen
maybe you aren't the one
Maybe you were
Maybe I wasn't

maybe they've all been the
one
at one point

and maybe there will
be
another
one.

If we think about it

They usually are the ones
that break our heart
its usually us
we tend to break our
own hearts
with made up realities
and thoughts
about them
about us

I broke my own heart
when I imagined
you as the person I want
and not as how you were.

A letter to you

I hope you are happy
I really do
I hope you get what you want in life
I hope you can do it
I hope you are strong enough
for what you want.

what we shared, i'll always cherish
the moments
as you called them
those moments with you
I'll always remember
and you
I'll always remember

Break ups

After my breakup
something changes in us
however much it takes
we somehow become better.

we can never be the person
we were before

I don't really know
how I was before you

Numb

There is no cure
for a broken heart
but time

but even time
won't fully heal it
it will just lead
to a place

a place where
it won't matter much

where we become more
numb to it.

Late night thoughts

I wonder
if we are still together
in another reality

Past or present

Past or present you have to decide
in which is fit for you to live
forever drowning in your memories
or more to gain in what you give

to lead a life and gain respect
thats worthy of your years
or forever looking backwards
suffocating in your fears

what you judge as failure
within yourself you must decide
when people rely on your decisions
don't turn your back or try to hide

how can you be aware
when your eyes are drawn to the ground
so many people past or present
their lives are lost or found

Regret

You stopped dreaming
and like a
bitter winter
regret set in.

Dark heart

Let me peel back
the layers of armour
that guard your dark heart
that is now ready to heal.

The Artist

Today there is silence in the museum of fine arts
a dreadful solemn and eerie hush and stillness
that bows its head in reverence to polite
conformity
aargh
we should be cheering and dancing wildly
celebrating the vibrancy of a life of colour
that the artists imagination has brought to his
canvas
this artist gave his life for you

Tempest of emotions

I will calm you like
a pale mist
slowly unfolding
before you surrender
to my tempest of emotions

A little hope

I am still hoping that
one day, one evening
in september
that you will text me
with one of your silly jokes
and how much you miss me

I do

Autumn is coming
and
I hope you are here
too

Time for us

I looked at the sky
last night and tried
to trace your name

after all this time
after all the people i've met
it's still you
it's all about you
                and I believe

                some day, one day
                there will be a time
                for us.

Be here

I don't want to
imagine you
being here anymore

I want you to
be here
with me
now.

Tell me all

Talk to me about the universe
      about your dreams
      about your fears

Tell me where you want to be, few years after
      what makes you happy
      what makes you sad

Tell me you'll be here.

Another outcome

I wish there is
a way to see
where another decision
would take us

where would we be
if we chose
something else

I wish we could see
like a little movie.

Anyone new

I don't know if I love you
but I don't like the thought
of anyone new

What it was

It was love at first sight
and she never left.

ask me about the day
we met and I'll
remember nothing but
the feeling I got

Jazz

Its jazz you know
another shade of blue
as a saxophone weeps
still searching for a note like you

I knew

In that one moment
caught between
the aroma of freshly baked pastries
and the distant sound of traffic
I knew that my life had changed forever
as I caught the man behind the counter
watching us
with a look of pure unbridled happiness
as he realised that he was witnessing
for the very first time
in his lifetime
the birth of a love so intense and powerful
that it would impact on the lives of millions
as poetry.

Bitterest pill

Evenings trails of
pink and tangerine
dissolve
along with the days
bitterest pill

Guess the former didn't matter after all

I've always had this idea
in my mind that
I'd meet a guy
with eyes as green
as emerald

then

I met you
with your eyes
the colour of charcoal
and I fell
too hard.

Your eyes

When I look into your eyes
I see further
than I have ever seen
before.

Search for happiness

We search for happiness
in the future
in foreign places
in people

without knowing

it's been within us all along.

Welcome stranger

Welcome stranger
said ambition
I've been waiting for you.

One moment

Happy endings
they tell us

It is not the ending
I want to be happy
whilst I am here

you only have now
just this one
moment.

Don't wake me up

You are my dream
and
I really don't want to
wake up.

from you

Do's and Don'ts

Don't ever go
searching for love

Do the things that
make you happy.

Years to come

Some say when you can't
be together then that
is love

I'd like to believe
I'd still love you
years to come

About love

We think we know
about love

we speak of it like
it's an old friend

we don't actually
know much about it

otherwise we would't
hurt it.

By night

They live by night
I live my dreams.

Breakfast date

I met you in the morning light
in the heat of summer
we had coffee and crepes
it was crowded but
all I could see was you

Stories

Tell me all of
your stories

before the morning comes
and I'll share with you mine
in the hopes that we'll
have stories to tell
others
together

It could've gone differently
but then it wouldn't be like this
we wouldn't be where we are now

Distant destinations

I can feel our hearts
beating paths to
distant destinations

An idea

I walked through
dreaming streets
holding hands with
an idea.

Paradise

I want white buildings with balconies
and the bright blue sea.

I want outside cafe bustling with happy
and carefree people, laughing.

I want ice cold drinks with purple straw
and very red strawberries.

I want golden sunshine with someone playing
the guitar outside and singing to the tune.

I want you there
with me.

True

I said goodbye to
fairytales
as soon as my dreams
started coming
true.

Merry go round

The night air permeates
sweet scented
lilac and honey suckle
dancing delicate barefoot
tip toeing whispers
under the watchful gaze
of towering guardian trees
carousel dreaming
of beating hearts
spinning breathless
on the merry go round tonight.

A town

In a town called
imagination
anything is possible.

You just know

You just know
when you see strangers
smiling at you
that they can see
what you are feeling

you just know
destiny and love
have made their entrance
just as they were meant to
on this day at this moment.

Your kisses

Your kisses taste
like the Paris
I had
always dreamed of.

Nowhere

There is a well worn path
leading to nowhere
where the memories
of excuses and discarded dreams
gather to discuss
their disappointments and regrets
where the whispering increases
in rhythmic and lyrical intensity
                if only I had
                I wish I had
                if only I had
                I wish I had.

Orchestra of my heart

Sing me that song again
the one that conducts
the orchestra of my heart.

Now

Back at the old house
in the lavender
scented garden
the memories are calling
reminding me of the promises
I once made
that my dreams
would not stay dreams
and that my thoughts and words
would make a difference
not just some day

but one day
now.

The place

This is the place of my dream
the place where my heart is poetry.

The blue bridge

Past the silver birch
and onto the blue bridge
over slowly ebbing waters
that catch sparkling reflections
like a distant halo of falling stars
this is the place where time stands still
so all my thoughts can return to you.

Adventures

I want to go on an adventure
I want to see the northern lights
with you on a cold evening.
when spring comes, I want to
ride the gondola in Venice with you
whilst wearing a long red dress.

I want to spend an afternoon
in a little cafe in Paris
drinking red wine until the sun goes down
and laughing at the silliest of things

I want a candle lit cocktails
on a rooftop under the shining stars

on a warm summer night in London

what I'm trying to say is
I don't mind wherever we are
I want you by my side.

Take my hand

Take my hand
it might be late now
but it maybe right, now

so take my hand
and lets go to the end
of the rainbow

take my hand
and lets live a life
painted on the ten of cups.

We met now
where I was yours
and you?
have always been mine.

You

I have seen so much
beauty in my life
but I have never felt
anything as beautiful as you

Love me in November

Love me when the year
is nearing to an end

love me when the beauty of
autumn is wearing off

love me when the golden leaves
on the trees are slowly dying

love me when the harshness of the
cold hits your face

love me with all my faults

if you love me
love me in November.

This feeling

Slow dance with me
to the other side of life
where this feeling
will never fade
or be forgotten

In Poetry

Home is not a place
it's a person, a feeling
I wasn't looking, for a person
to call home
but then I met you

It was like I've always known you
in that moment all the stars aligned
to form your name

I wrote waves of words to you
turning you into poetry
to keep you there forever

a poem of all the words that I hold
on a thread

truth is

in poetry
I found home
I saw you as poetry too.

If

If you are frightened of love

you are frightened of life

This is the moment

I am who I am
thats all I ever was
and who I will always be
and as the fairy lights
playfully reflect in your eyes
this is the moment we move closer
and take on this world together.

Always

For me
the rhythm of life
has always been
your heartbeat

The empty path

I will always turn away from the path
already lined with gold and silver
to walk the empty path with you.

this path will the be journey we create
and be full of the wonders and adventures
of our imaginations.

Stolen glance

A stolen glance
was the moment
when everything
changed

All this madness

Come fly with me
lets escape
all this madness
leave it all
behind us

come fly with me
say goodbye to this city
together we can build
a while new one

come fly with me
a new destination
never to return.

Just

    come

          fly

    with

me

Your heart

Does your heart
whisper my name
softly like a lullaby
or
scream it with
passion and desire

Wordsmith

She's a poem
a mystery, a riddle
waiting to be solved
and I tried to be a wordsmith

We all want something

I want to die
before you
so I don't have
to live
a life without you

Always met

As September slowly
went away and the
leaves turned a shade
of golden orange
I saw your face again
and it was like
we've always met

Mask

Like a sinking ship, a drama all at sea
through highs and lows, no one knows this life
of you
and me
washed up on an island, dried out in the sun
the jungles closing in on me, there's nowhere
left to run

ripples on a mill pond, a tidal wave at sea
whichever way I turn, life washes over me
swimming boy to drowning man, fighting against
the tide

washed up on the shore again, nowhere left to
hide

I look into a mirror, how could it be
I wanted to be you, but you ended as me
so I smash the mirror, at last I am free
to put another mask on, and be who I was
meant to be.

Young pretender

Not so much
the young pretender
more of a beautiful
kind of old

The dream

There is no better place
than the dream
where I found you

Don't look back

Caught in an unexpected landslide of charm
offensively so in my opinion
but what can you do
other than to feign indifference
and walk slowly away
don't look back
ever

Save yourself

You are your own hero

Today

I left yesterday, we couldn't
be together anymore

I'm yet to meet tomorrow

I'm with today, we are happy

Looking for you

I will look for you
in everyone
I meet

12pm

Today, I thought about you
at 12pm
I smiled remembering that
last night it was been
exactly three years since
I last saw you
I wondered where you were
I wondered if you thought about me

I thought about you
at 12pm
when the sun was out.

I don't want to

I would have got over you
a very long time ago
if I wanted to forget you
but I didn't want to
I really didn't
I don't

I don't want to be over you

The parts we'll miss out

"I'm good, thanks. You?"
Is what I will say
I'll miss out the parts;
Where I've missed you
                              a lot
                              I still do
that you're on my mind before I
fall asleep.
that you're my first thought
in the morning.
that I still flinch when I
hear your name.
that I tell strangers about
you.
that I still check your page
every so often.
that I write, rewrite and delete
words to you.

that, I love you.

"I'm good, thanks"
                you'll reply
            with the parts you've missed out.

Book of you

Everyone has got a story to tell
and mine is always you

About the Author

Elise Michael currently lives in London
but longs to live by the sea with a little dog
or two, where she could write all day.

Lots of love. Elise.

Printed in Great Britain
by Amazon